Ketanji Brown Jackson

From "Most Likely to Succeed" to the Supreme Court

by Jennifer Marino Walters

illustrated by Niall Harding

Red Chair Press   Egremont, Massachusetts

Look! Books are produced and published by Red Chair Press:

Red Chair Press LLC   PO Box 333   South Egremont, MA 01258-0333

www.redchairpress.com

 FREE lesson guide at www.redchairpress.com/free-activities

Publisher's Cataloging-In-Publication Data
(Provided by Cassidy Cataloguing Services, Inc.)
Names: Marino Walters, Jennifer, author. | Harding, Niall, illustrator.
Title: Ketanji Brown Jackson : from "Most Likely to Succeed" to the Supreme Court /
by Jennifer Marino Walters ; illustrated by Niall Harding.

Other titles: Look! books (Red Chair Press). Beginner biography

Description: Egremont, Massachusetts : Red Chair Press, [2024] | Includes index.
   | Interest age level: 006-009. | Summary: Born in Washington, DC, in 1970,
   and raised in Miami, Florida, Ketanji Brown Jackson developed an interest in
   law and politics at an early age. While in grade school, she sat with her father
   and watched him complete his law school assignments. And though some people,
   including a school guidance counselor, discouraged Ketanji from aiming high,
   she proved them wrong and graduated with honors from Harvard Law School
   after being named in high school as Most Likely to Succeed. She went on to serve
   on the U.S. District Court and the United States Court of Appeals before making
   history and becoming the first Black woman to be confirmed to the United States
   Supreme Court in 2022.--Publisher.

Identifiers: ISBN: 9781643713670 (library hardcover) | 9781643713687 (paperback)
   | 9781643713694 (multiuser ebook) | LCCN: 2023935432

Subjects: LCSH: Jackson, Ketanji Brown, 1970---Juvenile literature. | United
   States. Supreme Court-- Officials and employees--Biography--Juvenile literature.
   | African American women judges-- Biography--Juvenile literature. | CYAC:
   Jackson, Ketanji Brown, 1970- | United States. Supreme Court--Officials and
   employees--Biography. | African American women judges-- Biography. | LCGFT:
   Biographies. | BISAC: JUVENILE NONFICTION / Biography & Autobiography
   / Women. | JUVENILE NONFICTION / Biography & Autobiography / Political.
   | JUVENILE NONFICTION / Biography & Autobiography / Cultural, Ethnic &
   Regional.

Classification: LCC: KF8745.J25 W35 2024 | DDC: 347.732634--dc23

Photo credits: Fred Schilling, Collection of the Supreme Court of the United States

Printed in the United States of America

0324 1P CGF24

Table of Contents

Lovely One

Ketanji Onyika Brown was born on September 14, 1970 in Washington, D.C. Ketanji (keh-THAN-jee) means "lovely one" in Swahili, an African language. Her parents—both schoolteachers—wanted their daughter's name to represent their African **ancestry**.

Ketanji's parents grew up during
a time when Black people did
not have the same rights as
white people. There were laws
that required Blacks and whites
to be segregated (separated)
in schools and in many public
places. Those laws were removed
by the end of the 1960s.

A Bright Future

When Ketanji was 4 years old, the family moved to Miami, Florida so her father could attend law school. Little Ketanji loved to sit with her dad and color in her coloring books while he read his law books. That was when she first became interested in law.

In Ketanji's Words
"My parents… taught me hard work. They taught me **perseverance**. They taught me that anything is possible in this great country."
–Ketanji to Senator Cory Booker in 2022

Ketanji's mother became
a high school principal. Ketanji's
parents taught her that she
could do anything, no matter
the color of her skin.

Star Student

When Ketanji started school, she worked hard and got very good grades. In middle school, she was **elected** school mayor. In high school, she was elected student-body president three times.

Good to Know

According to her high school yearbook, Ketanji's classmates voted her "most talented" and "most likely to succeed."

8

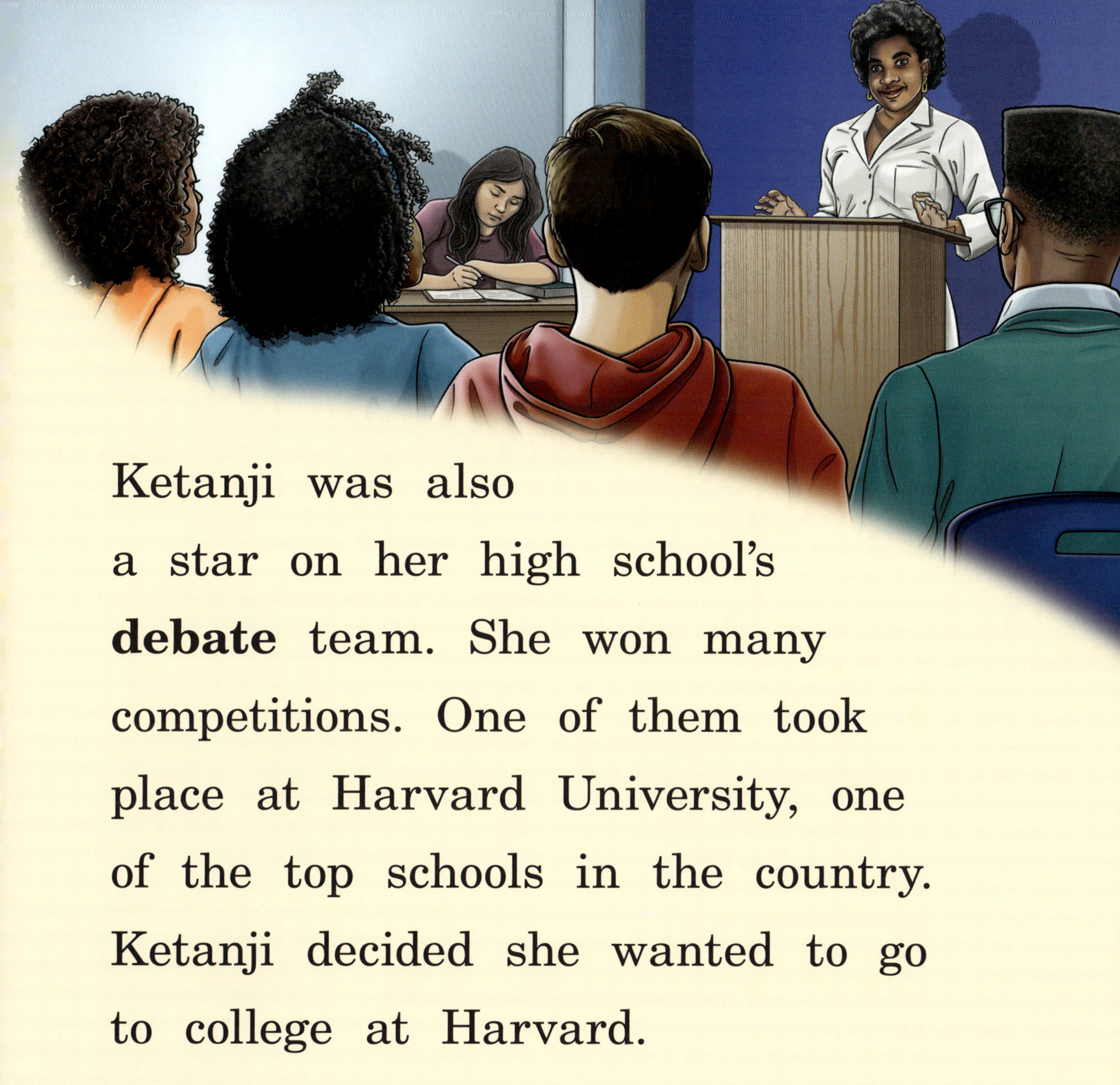

Ketanji was also
a star on her high school's
debate team. She won many
competitions. One of them took
place at Harvard University, one
of the top schools in the country.
Ketanji decided she wanted to go
to college at Harvard.

Ketanji's guidance counselor told her not to aim so high. But Ketanji didn't listen. She applied to Harvard anyway—and got in.

Ketanji graduated from Harvard with honors in 1992. She then went to Harvard Law School. She graduated from there with honors in 1996.

Good to Know

Ketanji is only the second **generation** in her family to go to college.

A Budding Career

That's when Ketanji's law career began. She worked as a clerk (assistant) for two U.S. judges, and then for Supreme Court Justice Stephen Breyer. She then held several other law jobs.

From 2005 to 2007, Ketanji worked as a public defender. That meant she helped prisoners and other people accused of crimes who could not afford to pay for a lawyer.

Ketanji joined the U.S. District Court in 2012 and the U.S. Court of Appeals in 2021. They are both very important courts in the country.

Big Nomination

In January 2022, Justice Breyer announced that he would retire from the Supreme Court that summer. President Biden thought long and hard about who he wanted to replace Justice Breyer. He decided to **nominate** Ketanji. It was a huge honor.

"I can only hope that my life and career, my love of this country and the Constitution… will inspire future generations of Americans," Ketanji said.

In April 2022, the Senate confirmed Ketanji's nomination.

Making History

Ketanji was sworn in as a U.S. Supreme Court Justice on June 30, 2022. It was a historic moment: Ketanji became the first Black woman ever to serve on the Supreme Court. She also became the first Supreme Court Justice to have ever been a public defender. And she was the first-ever Justice from the state of Florida.

Good to Know

Ketanji is only the third Black Supreme Court Justice. The first, Thurgood Marshall, served on the Court from 1967–1991. The second, Clarence Thomas, joined the Supreme Court in 1991.

17

Diversity in the Court

When Ketanji joined the Supreme Court, it also marked the first time that four women were on the Court at the same time. Ketanji joined Justices Sonia Sotomayor, Elena Kagan, and Amy Coney Barrett.

Good to Know

Sandra Day O'Connor was the first woman to become a Supreme Court Justice. She served on the Court from 1981–2006. The second was Ruth Bader Ginsburg, who served from 1993 until her death in 2020.

And with Clarence Thomas
serving on the Court, it became
the first time in history that
white men did not make up the
majority of the Supreme Court.

A Role Model

As a Supreme Court Justice, Ketanji has vowed to be fair when making decisions. She remains a role model for girls, especially her daughters, Talia and Leila. They were born in 2000 and 2004.

In Ketanji's Words

"Girls like my daughters need to learn that they have opportunities in America today; opportunities that don't exist for girls in many other countries."
—from a 2017 speech

In March 2023, a street in Cutler Bay, Florida (the town near Miami where Ketanji grew up) was renamed in her honor. It is now called Justice Ketanji Brown Jackson Street.

Timeline: Big Dates in Ketanji's Life

1970: Ketanji is born in Washington, D.C.

1974: Ketanji and her family move to a town near Miami, Florida, where she grows up.

1992: She graduates with honors from Harvard University.

1996: Ketanji graduates with honors from Harvard Law School and marries Patrick Jackson.

February 2022: President Joe Biden nominates Ketanji to the U.S. Supreme Court.

April 2022: The U.S. Senate confirms Ketanji's nomination.

June 2022: Ketanji becomes the first Black woman ever to serve on the Supreme Court.

2023: A street in Cutler Bay, Florida is renamed in Ketanji's honor.

Words to Know

ancestry: family background

debate: a discussion which people give different opinions about a topic

elected: chosen for a job or position through voting

generation: the people in a family born and living during the same time

majority: more than half of something

nominate: choose as a candidate for a job or position

perseverance: a quality in which someone continues to try to do something even though it's very difficult

Learn More at the Library

(Check out these books to read with others)

Charles, Tami. *Ketanji Brown Jackson: A Justice for All.* Simon & Schuster Books for Young Readers, 2023.

Magoon, Kekla. *Ketanji.* Harper Quill Tree. 2023.

Moses, Shelia P. *Who Is Ketanji Brown Jackson?* Penguin Workshop, 2022.

Schwartz, Heather E. *Ketanji Brown Jackson: First Black Woman on the U.S. Supreme Court.* Lerner Publications, 2023.

Index

About the Author

Jennifer Marino Walters lives with her twin boys and daughter in Virginia near Washington D.C. Jennifer is proud that her children have role models like Justice Jackson to inspire them to be their best.